GCSE

Questions and Answers

Q&A

MATHEMATICS

KEY STAGE 4

Mark Patmore Principal Examiner
Brian Seager Chief Examiner

Letts
EDUCATIONAL

SERIES EDITOR: BOB McDUELL

Contents

HOW TO USE THIS BOOK

The purpose of the *Questions and Answers* series is to help you achieve the grades you want in your GCSEs. This book is designed to help all students aiming for grades up to and including grade B and also provides a good basis for revision for the Standard Grade of the Scottish Certificate of Education, General Level. If you are aiming for a grade A or A* at GCSE, you will find additional questions focused specifically on this area in *Letts* GCSE *Questions and Answers Mathematics to A**.

This book is based on the idea that an experienced Examiner can give, through exam questions, sample answers and advice, the help you need to secure success. Many revision aids concentrate on providing the facts which might have to be remembered in an exam. This book focuses on giving you invaluable practice at doing exam questions, so that you can learn to improve your exam technique.

The *Questions and Answers* series is designed to provide:

● Easy to use **Revision Summaries** which identify the important facts. These are to remind you, in summary form, of the topics you will need to have revised in order to answer exam questions. (Answers to the illustrative examples are also provided.)

● Advice on the different types of question in each subject and how to answer them well to obtain the highest marks.

● Many examples of **exam questions**, with spaces for you to fill in your answers, just as in an exam. It is best if you try the questions first before going to the answers and the advice which accompanies them. The questions are either official Exam Board questions or have been specially written by experienced Examiners who write questions for the Exam Boards.

● **Sample answers** to all of the questions.

● **Examiner's tips.** By using the experience of Examiners we are able to give advice on how your answers can be improved, and how common mistakes can be avoided.

THE IMPORTANCE OF USING QUESTIONS FOR REVISION

Past exam questions play an important part in revising for exams. However, it is important not to start practising questions too early. Nothing can be more disheartening than trying to do a question that you do not understand because you have not mastered the concepts. Therefore it is important to have studied a topic thoroughly before attempting questions on it.

It is unlikely that any question you try will appear in exactly the same form on the papers you are going to take. However the number of totally original questions that can be set on any part of the syllabus is limited and so similar ideas occur over and over again. It certainly will help you if the question you are trying to answer in an exam is familiar and you are used to the type of language used. Your confidence will be boosted, and confidence is important for exam success.

Practising exam questions will also highlight gaps in your knowledge and understanding that you can go back and revise more thoroughly.

Finally, having access to answers, as you do in this book, will enable you to see clearly what is required by the examiner, how best to answer each question and the amount of detail required.

MAXIMISING YOUR MARKS IN MATHEMATICS

One of the keys to exam success is to know how marks are gained or lost and the examiner's tips given with the solutions in this book give hints on how you can maximise your marks on particular questions. However you should also take careful note of these general points:

- Check the requirements of your exam board and follow the instructions (or 'rubric') carefully. Many Mathematics papers start with short, straightforward questions. You should work through them in order so that you build up your confidence. Do not overlook any parts of a question – double-check that you have seen everything, including any questions on the back page! Take time to read through all the questions carefully, and then start with the question you think you can do best.

- Get into the habit of setting out your work neatly and logically. If you are untidy and disorganised you could penalise yourself by misreading your own figures or lose marks because your method is not obvious. Always show all necessary working so that you can obtain marks for a correct method even if your final answer is wrong. Remember that a good clear sketch can help you to see important details.

- When the question asks for a particular result to be established, remember that to obtain the method marks you must show sufficient working to convince the examiner that your argument is valid.

- Do rough estimates of calculations to make sure that they are reasonable, state units if applicable and give answers to the required degree of accuracy; do not approximate too early in your working.

- Make sure that you are familiar with the formulas at the front of the exam paper and learn any useful formulas that are not included.

- When about 15 minutes remain, check whether you are running short of time. If so, try to score as many marks as possible in the short time that remains, concentrating on the easier parts of any questions not yet tackled.

- The following glossary may help you in answering questions:
  Write down, state – no explanation is needed for an answer.
  Calculate, find, show, solve – include enough working to make your method clear.
  Draw – plot accurately, using graph paper and selecting a suitable scale; this is usually preparation for reading information from the graph.

DIFFERENT TYPES OF EXAM QUESTION

There are different types of question which appear on exam papers. Questions on Mathematics papers are of two types:

'Pure' Mathematics Questions
These are usually short and are focused on one particular skill or part of the syllabus.

Example 1: Solve the equation $2x - 3 = 42 - 3x$.

Answer _____ (2)

Structured Questions

These are the most common type of question in GCSE Mathematics papers and thus most of the questions in this book are structured questions. These questions usually have a context – that is they are about the application of mathematics to a real (or nearly real!) situation.

In a structured question, the question is divided into parts (a), (b), (c) etc. These parts may be further subdivided into (i), (ii) and so on. A structure is built into the question and, hence, into your answer. Frequently, answers from one part of a question are used in subsequent parts, but an error in, say, part (a), which may result in few, or even no, marks being obtained for that part should not result in no marks being obtained in subsequent parts, provided the incorrect answer is used 'correctly'. There are numbers in brackets, e.g. (3), to show how many marks are allocated to the various parts of a question.

Example 2:   The diagram shows the design for a company's logo which is to be painted on the side of a building.

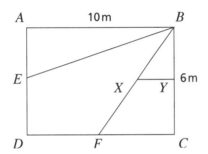

The design is a rectangle, *ABCD*, 10 m long and 6 m wide. *E*, the midpoint of *AD*, and *F*, the midpoint of *DC*, are joined to *B*. *XY* is the line joining the midpoints of *BF* and *BC*.

(a) Calculate the area of triangle *ABE*.

Answer _____ m² (2)

(b) Calculate the area of triangle *BFC*.

Answer _____ m² (2)

(c) Hence calculate the area of quadrilateral *BEDF*.

Answer _____ m² (1)

Answers to examples:

1: $x = 9$
2: (a) 15 m²   (b) 15 m²   (c) 30 m²

1 Number

Questions asked in Number, and the knowledge and skills required to answer them fall into three broad categories.

The first is **calculation** and is relatively straightforward. Questions here will involve the manipulation of numbers – the 4 rules ($+$, $-$, $\times$, $\div$) – and the use of calculators. At the lower levels questions such as:

> Example 1: Find the cost of 75 calculators at £8.49 each.

> Example 2: A washing machine has its price reduced from £325 to £280 in a sale. Calculate the percentage reduction.

may be set. At the higher levels the questions may include topics such as standard form:

> Example 3: If $x = 1.4 \times 10^{-3}$ and $y = 4.6 \times 10^4$ find, in standard form,
> (a) $x \times y$, and (b) $x \div y$.

> Example 4: A clock ticks every half second. How many times will it tick in a year?

Substitution into a formula may be required:

> Example 5: If $\dfrac{1}{f} = \dfrac{1}{u} + \dfrac{1}{v}$ find f when $u = 2$ and $v = 3$.

> Example 6: Find the value of s when
> $$s = ut + \tfrac{1}{2}at^2, u = 7.83, t = 6, a = -0.64$$

The next group of questions are concerned with **estimation**, **approximation** and **errors**.

Questions involving **estimation** may ask for answers to be checked and/or justified.

> Example 7: Show that the value of $\dfrac{17.8 \times 0.53}{0.238}$ is roughly 40.

This is a useful way to check all work on the calculator.

Questions involving **approximation** could include some which asked for answers to be rounded to appropriate degrees of accuracy as well as those involving calculations using approximate numbers. **Errors** arise in questions where, for example, measurements to a given degree of accuracy are involved.

> Example 8: 27.3 is correct to 3 significant figures. Write the upper and lower bounds.

> Example 9: Cards are made with width 160 mm, to the nearest 5 mm. Envelopes are made with width 162 mm, to nearest millimetre. Will a card always fit in an envelope? Explain your answer.

If you need to revise this subject more thoroughly, see the relevant topics in the _Letts_ GCSE _Mathematics_ _Study Guide_ or _CD-ROM._

Answers to examples:

1: £636.75   2: 13.8%   3: (a) 6.44×10 (b) 3.04×10^{-8}
4: 63 072 000 or 6.3072×10^7 5: 1.2   6: 35.46
8: 27.25 and 27.35   9: Smallest envelope measures 161.5; largest card measures 162.5. It may not fit.

1 Mrs Jones bought 40 scientific calculators costing £7.30 each and some graphical calculators costing £36.80 each. Altogether she spent £733.60. How many graphical calculators did she buy?

....

Answer _____ (2)

2 During the first 3 weeks of life a baby increases its weight from 3.6 kg to 4.7 kg. What is the percentage increase?

....

Answer _____% (2)

3 There are about 7000 cinemas in the UK. Every day about 400 people visit each one. The population of the UK is about 60 million. About what percentage of the population visit a cinema each day?

....

Answer _____% (2)

4 A car manufacturer reduces the prices of its hatchback from £12 800 to £12 400. What is the percentage reduction?

....

Answer _____ % (2)

5 If $V = IR$, what is the percentage increase in V when I increases by 10% and R increases by 20%?

....

Answer _____ % (4)

6 If $P = \sqrt{\dfrac{V}{Q}}$, find P when $V = 4.6 \times 10^6$ and $Q = 2.8 \times 10^2$. Give your answer in standard form.

....

Answer $P =$ _____ (2)

7 The land area of the Earth's surface is about 4×10^{11} km^2. The population of the Earth is approximately 5000 million.

(a) Write the population of the Earth in standard form.

Answer _____ (1)

(b) Calculate the approximate average area, in km^2 per head of population. Give your answer in standard form.

....

Answer _____ km^2 (2)

8 Calculate:

(a) $\dfrac{26.78 \times 0.0831}{15.3 \times 6.81}$

(i) Show all the digits on your calculator display.

Answer _____ (2)

(ii) Round your answer to a sensible degree of accuracy.

Answer _____ (1)

(b) $\dfrac{15.32 + 9.07}{15.32 - 9.07}$

Show all the digits.

Answer _____ (2)

9 Henry bought some furniture. It cost £1750.

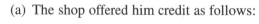

(a) The shop offered him credit as follows:

Repayment over 12 months

Cash	10% deposit	Monthly payments	Total credit price
1750.00	175.00	147.00	1939.00

He paid the 10% deposit. What is the rate of interest on the amount to be repaid?

....

Answer _____% (2)

(b) He could have paid back the money over 2 years:

Repayment over 24 months

Cash	10% deposit	Monthly payments	Total credit price
1750.00	175.00	81.37	2127.88

Show how you can **estimate** whether this is the same rate of interest per year.

.... (2)

10 I have a small packet to post. To find out how much it will cost, I weigh it.

(a) First I weigh it on scales that weigh to the nearest 10 g.
   The packet weighs 70 g.

   Write down the smallest that the weight of the packet could be.

   Answer _____ g (1)

(b) Now I weigh it on electronic scales where the display goes up in 5 g intervals.
   The packet weighs 65 g.

   Write down the upper and lower bounds of the weight of the package according to the
   electronic scales.

   Upper bound .... g   Lower bound .... g   (2)

(c) Finally, I weigh it on a balance to the nearest gram.
   It weighs 62 g.

   Can all the scales be right? Explain.

   .... (2)

11 The formula

$$s = \frac{v^2 - u^2}{2a}$$

gives the distance travelled in metres when the velocity changes from u m/s to v m/s due to a
constant acceleration of a m/s^2.

Find s when $v = 25.0$
                     $u = 50.0$
                     $a = -9.8$

....

                     Answer $s =$ _____ m (3)

12 (a)

Leaded petrol	52.4p per litre
Unleaded petrol	49.6p per litre

I filled the petrol tank of my car with unleaded petrol. It cost me £18.60.

(i) How many litres did I buy?

....

.... (2)

(ii) How much more would it have cost me if I had bought leaded petrol instead?

....

.... (2)

(b) Last year the amounts I spent on road tax, car insurance and petrol were in the ratio 1: 3: 7.

I spent a total of £1430 on these three items.

Calculate how much I spent on petrol.

....

.... (2)

NEAB 1995

13 Mr Clark borrowed £650 on 1 January 1990. He repaid £243 on 31 December 1990 and the same amount each succeeding 31 December. Compound interest was charged at 6% per annum on the balance during the year. How much was left to pay after 31 December 1992?

....

Answer £ _____ (3)

14 (a) Megan is 5 feet 3 inches tall.

1 cm = 0.394 inches.
12 inches = 1 foot.

Calculate Megan's height in centimetres.
Give your answer to an appropriate degree of accuracy.

....

Answer _____ cm (2)

(b) An electronic weighing scale gives Megan's weight as 63.4792kg.
Give her weight correct to an appropriate degree of accuracy.

Answer _____ kg (1)

SEG 1995

15 For safety, the maximum a caravan should weigh is 85% of the tow car.
The Keenan's family car weighs 1124 kg.

(a) Find, to the nearest kg, the maximum weight of the caravan that the Keenan's car can tow within the 85% limit.

....

Answer _____ kg (3)

Here are the weights of four caravans P, Q, R, and S.

P
19.2 cwt

Q
15.4 cwt

R
17.3 cwt

S
20.4 cwt

One hundredweight (1 cwt) is equal to 50.8 kg (to 1 decimal place).

(b) Work out which of the four caravans the Keenan's car could tow within the 85% limit.
Show clearly how you decided.

....

....

Answer _____ (4)

The Jones's family car weighs 1220 kg and their caravan weighs 1030 kg.

(c) Work out what percentage the caravan is of the car's weight and state whether it is within the 85% limit.

....

Answer _____ %

Within limit (Yes/No) _____ (4)

ULEAC 1995

9

16 Sheena weighs 8 stones 6 pounds.

There are 14 pounds in a stone and 1 kilogram is equal to 0.157 stones.

Change Sheena's weight into kilograms.

Give your answer to an appropriate degree of accuracy.

....

....

....

Answer _____ kg   (4)

SEG 1995

17 (a) When going on holiday to Italy, Joe exchanged £200 for 520 000 Italian lira.

    (i) Pat changed £300 into lira at the same exchange rate.
        How many lira did Pat receive?

....

....

Answer _____ lira   (3)

    (ii) Joe actually spent $\frac{7}{8}$ of his lira.

        How many lira did he **not** spend?

....

....

Answer _____ lira   (3)

(b) Samantha came to England from the USA for a holiday. She changed her dollars ($) into pounds (£) at the rate $1 = £0.68.

At Heathrow airport, Samantha bought a T shirt for £12.99.

What was the cost, in dollars, of the T shirt?

....

Answer $ _____   (2)

MEG 1995

Questions asked in algebra and the knowledge and skills required to answer them fall into three broad categories.

The first is **number patterns and sequences**. It will be necessary to find rules which enable you to continue a number pattern such as 1, 3, 6, 10, 15, ... in words or symbols.

Example 1: Find the nth terms of these sequences.
(a) 2, 4, 6, 8, 10, ...
(b) 1, 3, 5, 7, 9, ...
(c) 2, 8, 18, 32, 50, ...

The next group of questions is the largest and involves **solving equations and algebraic manipulation**. At the simplest level it will be necessary to solve equations such as:

Example 2: (a) $5x - 3 = 3 - x$ or (b) $x^2 = 27$

the latter by the method of 'trial and improvement'. More complex equations will also be set. An equation such as

Example 3: $x^2 + 2x = 7$

can also be solved by trial and improvement. Graphical methods may also be used, possibly associated with other mathematics. Equations like

Example 4: $2x - y = 9$
$x + 3y = 8$

may be solved by graphical or algebraic methods. In addition to equations, inequalities must also be solved. These can range from listing whole numbers which satisfy, for example:

Example 5: $-2 < n \leqslant 6$

to finding values of x and y which satisfy

Example 6: $x > 7, y \geqslant 4, x + y \leqslant 20$

Again, solution by graphical or algebraic methods may be required. Such solutions will involve algebraic manipulation but the factorizing of expressions such as

Example 7: (a) $ax^2 + 2bx$ or (b) $x^2 - 3x - 10$

will occur either as part of a longer question or on their own. Expanding, (multiplying out brackets), is another skill that could be required and 'changing the subject' of a formula is a regular requirement.

Example 8: make a the subject of $v = u + at$

The last group is concerned with **graphical representation**. The use of coordinates is expected at all levels and this may involve graphical solutions as already mentioned. The interpretation of graphs of simple functions and also those which represent physical situations, such as speed/time, will be asked.

If you need to revise this subject more thoroughly, see the relevant topics in the *Letts* GCSE *Mathematics Study Guide* or *CD-ROM*.

Answers to examples:

1: (a) $2n$ (b) $2n - 1$ (c) $2n^2$

2: (a) $x = 1$ (b) $x = 5.2$ or -5.2

3: $x = 1.8$ or -3.8

4: $x = 5, y = 1$

5: $-1, 0, 1, 2, 3, 4, 5, 6$

6: many answers possible, for example if $x = 8$ then y would lie between 4 and 12.

7: (a) $x(ax + 2b)$ (b) $(x - 5)(x + 2)$

8: $a = \dfrac{v - u}{t}$

1 The first 3 terms of a sequence are:

$(3 \times 4) + 1,$ $(4 \times 5) + 2,$ $(5 \times 6) + 3.$

(a) Write down the next term.

.... (1)

(b) Write down the 6th term.

.... (1)

(c) Write down the nth term, and simplify your answer.

.... (3)

2 Look at this sequence

$$3, \ 6, \ 11, \ 18, \ 27, \ ...$$

(a) (i) Write down the next two terms in the sequence.

....

Answer _____ (1)

(ii) Explain how you would find the next term.

.... (1)

(b) Find an expression for the nth term of

(i) $1, \ 4, \ 9, \ 16, \ 25, \ ...$

....

Answer _____ (1)

(ii) $3, \ 6, \ 11, \ 18, \ 27, \ ...$

....

Answer _____ (2)

3 Look at the three sequences below.

Sequence p 4, 6, 8, 10, 12, ...

Sequence q 3, 8, 15, 24, 35, ...

Sequence r 5, 10, 17, ...

(a) The sequence r is obtained from sequences p and q as follows.

$$\sqrt{4^2 + 3^2} = 5 \qquad \sqrt{6^2 + 8^2} = 10 \qquad \sqrt{8^2 + 15^2} = 17 \qquad \text{and so on.}$$

(i) Use the numbers 10 and 24 to calculate the fourth term of sequence r.

....

.... (2)

(ii) Calculate the fifth term of sequence r.

....

.... (2)

(b) (i) Find the tenth term of sequence p.

.... (1)

(ii) Find the sixth term of sequence q.

.... (1)

(c) (i) Write down the nth term of sequence p.

....

.... (2)

(ii) The nth term of sequence q is

$$n^2 + kn$$

where k represents a number.

Find the value of k.

.... (1)

NEAB 1995

4 (a) Multiply out the brackets and simplify the expression $(2x + 7)(3x - 6)$.

....

Answer _____ (2)

(b) (i) Factorize $x^2 + x - 6$.

....

(ii) Solve the equation $x^2 + x - 6 = 0$.

....

Answer $x =$ _____ (4)

5 Solve the equations:

(a) $11 - 3x = 4x - 10$,

....

Answer $x =$ _____ (3)

(b) $x^3 = 7$.
Use trial and improvement and show all your trials. Give your answer correct to 2
decimal places.

....

Answer $x =$ _____ (4)

6 (a) List the integer values of n for which $-2 < n \leqslant 5$.

....

....

Answer _____ (3)

(b) Express as simply as possible $\quad \dfrac{4x^2 \times 6x^5}{12x^3}$

....

....

Answer _____ (3)

(c) Simplify $(3y - 4)(5y + 6) + 10$.

....

....

Answer _____ (3)

MEG 1995

7 John and Sayed are playing a number game:

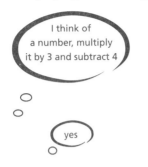

Let *n* be the number John thought of.

(a) Write down the inequality using *n*.

Answer _____ (1)

(b) Solve the inequality.

....

Answer _____ (2)

8 The graph of $3y = 2x + 3$ has been drawn on the grid.

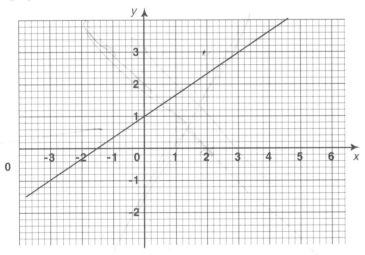

(a) On the same grid draw the graphs of (i) $y = 2x - 2$, (ii) $y = 3 - x$

....

.... (3)

(b) Use the graphs to solve the simultaneous equations $3y = 2x + 3$

$$y = 3 - x$$

Answer $x = $ _____

Answer $y = $ _____ (1)

9 Solve the simultaneous equations: $2x + 3y = 17$
$3x - 2y = 6.$

....

....

Answer $x =$ _____ $y =$ _____ (4)

10 The sum of the squares of the integers from 1 to n is given by

$$s = \tfrac{1}{6} n (n + 1)(2n + 1).$$

Find s when $n = 10$.

....

Answer $s =$ _____ (2)

11

The traffic capacity of a road can be found by using the following formula:

$$Q = \frac{3600VN}{C}$$

Q = number of vehicles per hour
V = average speed in m/s
N = number of lanes
C = optimum distance between vehicles

(a) Find the capacity of a 2 lane road where the average speed is 12 m/s and the optimum distance is 55 m.

....

Answer $Q =$ _____ (2)

(b) How many lanes will be needed through a tunnel which will have to take 1000 vehicles an hour, travelling at 15m/s with a spacing of 120 m?

....

Answer $N =$ _____ (3)

12 To change from Fahrenheit to Celsius we use the formula:

$$C = \tfrac{5}{9} (F - 32)$$

John claims that, on a hot day, the Fahrenheit reading can be exactly double the Celsius reading. At what temperature, Celsius, would this be true?

....

....

Answer _____ °C (4)

13 The mean and the median of the following numbers are equal. Find x.

30, 40, x, 50, 80.

....

....

Answer $x = $ _____ (5)

14 The *Better Diary Service* supply two kinds of desk diary, the *Page per Day* (PPD) and the *Page per Week* (PPW).
These are two of the orders:

| 3 PPD | 7 PPW | Total cost | £53.40 |
| 1 PPD | 10 PPW | Total cost | £50.00 |

Let d be the price of one PPD in £
    w be the price of one PPW in £.

(a) Write down two equations in d and w.

.... (2)

(b) Solve the equations to find the cost of each diary.

....

....

Answer PPD .... PPW .... (4)

15 Write down all the whole numbers (integers), n, which satisfy

$$-1 < n \leqslant 3.$$

.... (2)

16 Solve the equations

(a) $3x + 2 = 16$,

....

QUESTIONS

....

.... (2)

(b) $5(2x - 1) = 35,$

....

....

....

.... (2)

(c) $4x + 3 = 18 - 2x.$

....

....

....

.... (2)

NEAB 1996

17

An old formula gives the distance D miles that can be seen to the horizon when the observer is at height h feet above the sea. The radius of the Earth is r miles and is equal to 3950.

$$D = \sqrt{\frac{2rh}{5280}}$$

Find h when $D = 20$.

....

....

Answer $h =$ _____ feet (3)

18 Boyle's Law can be stated by the formula

$$P = \frac{k}{V}$$

where P is the pressure and V the volume of a gas.
Transform the formula to make V the subject.

.... (2)

19 Solve the inequalities

(a) $2x - 7 \leqslant 8$.

....

Answer _____ (1)

(b) $3 - x > 2$.

....

Answer_____ (1)

(c) $x^2 - 4 < 0$.

....

Answer _____ (2)

20 Use a trial and improvement method to solve the equation

$$x^3 - x = 15.$$

Complete the working below and find a solution correct to one decimal place.

x	$x^3 - x =$	
$x = 2$	$2^3 - 2 = 6$	Too small
$x = 3$	$3^3 - 3 = 24$	Too big

Answer $x =$ _____ (3)

ULEAC 1996

21 I want to make a regular octagon. Each side will be 14 cm. I shall make it from a square piece of card, by cutting off the four corners.

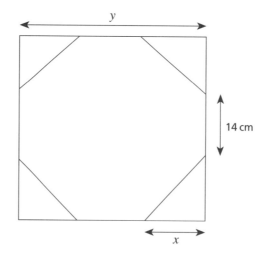

(a) Write down an expression for the area of the octagon in terms of x and y.

....

Answer Area = _____ (2)

(b) Use Pythagoras to find the value of x.

....

....

Answer $x =$ _____ (3)

(c) Find the area of the octagon.

....

....

Answer Area = _____ cm² (2)

22 (a) Solve the equation $3x - 2 = x + 7$

....

Answer $x =$ _____ (2)

(b) Solve the simultaneous equations

$$x + y = 4$$
$$15x + 25y = 76$$

....

....

....

Answer $x =$ _____ , $y =$ _____ (3)

(c) Solve the inequality $\qquad$ $2(3x - 2) < 11$

....

Answer _____ (2)

(d) Label with the letter R, the single region which satisfies all of these inequalities.

$$y > 2, \quad x + y > 4, \quad 0 < x < 3$$

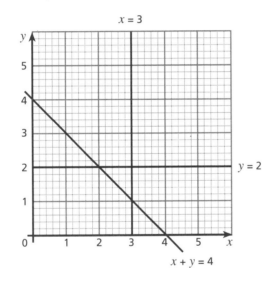

(1)

SEG 1995

23 This graph shows the speed of a cyclist as she rides along a hilly road.

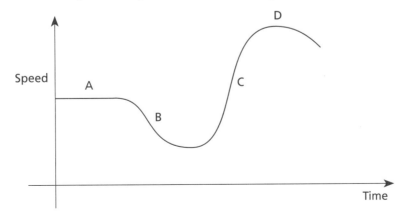

Describe what is happening at A, B, C, D.

A: ....

B: ....

C: ....

D: .... (4)

24 The graph represents a swimming race between Robert and James.

Robert

James

Distance from start (m)

Time (seconds)

(a) At what time did James overtake Robert for the second time?

Answer _____ seconds (1)

(b) What was the **maximum** distance between the swimmers during the race?

Answer _____ m (1)

(c) Who was swimming faster at 56 seconds? How can you tell?

.... (1)

SEG 1995

25 On the axes below draw the graphs of

(a) $y = 4 - x$

(b) $y = x^2$

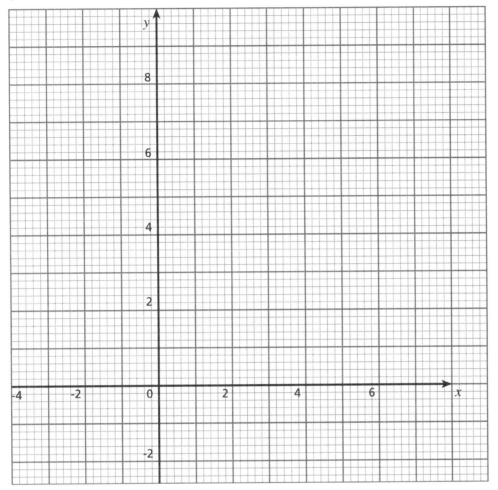

(3)

(c) (i) Write down the values of x where the graphs meet.

Answer $x =$ _____ (2)

(ii) Use trial and improvement to find these solutions correct to 2 decimal places.

....

....

....

Answer $x =$ _____ (4)

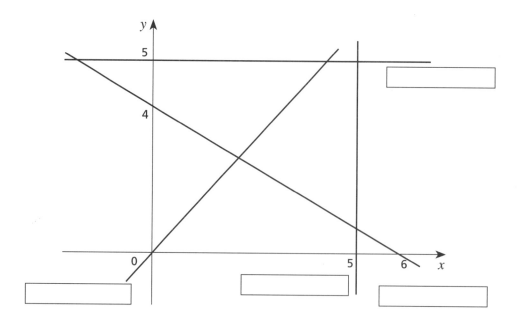

Four lines are drawn on the graph:

$$x = 5, \quad y = 5, \quad 2x + 3y = 12, \quad 2y = 3x.$$

(a) Label the lines by writing the correct equation in each box. (2)

(b) Show, by shading, the region which satisfies

$$x < 5, \quad y < 5, \quad 2x + 3y > 12, \quad 2y < 3x.$$ (2)

27 Match each description to a possible sketch graph. In each case label the axes.

A: $y = x^2$ B: $y = x^3$ C: $y = \dfrac{1}{x}$ D: $y + x = 3$

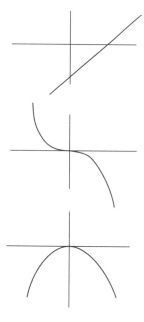
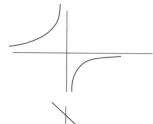
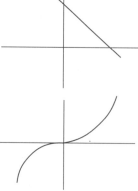
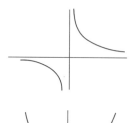
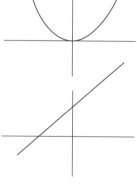

(4)

28

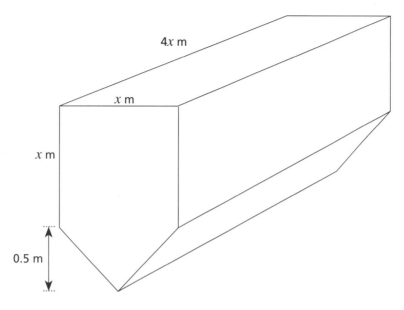

The diagram represents a grain hopper. The hopper is of length $4x$ metres and has a constant cross-section comprised of a square of side x metres and a triangle of perpendicular height 0.5 metres.

(a) Find, in terms of x, the area of the cross-section.

....

....

Answer _____ (3)

The hopper can hold 10 m^3 of grain.

(b) Show that $4x^3 + x^2 = 10$.

....

....

.... (3)

(c) Use a trial and improvement method to find the value of x, to one decimal place, for which $4x^3 + x^2 = 10$.

....

....

....

Answer $x =$ _____ (4)

NICCEA 1995

3 Shape and space

There are three main groups of questions in this attainment target plus some other types of question at the higher levels.

The first group is those concerned with **Pythagoras' Theorem and trigonometry in 2-D and 3-D shapes**.

Here questions such as:

> Example 1: Find the length of the sides *AC* and *AB* and the size of the angle *BCA* in the following triangle.

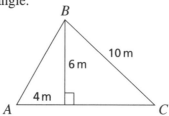

could appear but are often set in a context.

The next group involves the calculation of **areas and volumes of 2-D and 3-D shapes**.

You are expected to know the formulae for the area and circumference of a circle ($A = \pi r^2$, $C = 2\pi r$ or πd) and will be given the formulae for the areas and volumes of shapes such as the trapezium, cone and sphere.

> Example 2: A child's clown toy is made from a cone attached to a hemisphere of radius 5 cm. If the total height of the toy is 20 cm find its volume.

The third group of questions are those concerned with **position** and **locus**. These will include bearings – to define direction – and the use of coordinates in two and three dimensions to locate position.

> Example 3: A cuboid has its edges parallel to the axes. Its dimensions are 3, 2, 1 units. One vertex is at (2, 3, 0). Find a possible position for the opposite vertex.

> Example 4: Jane rows her boat under a bridge.
> She keeps the same distance from two bridge supports, *A* and *B*.
> Describe the locus of the boat.

The final – mixed – group will include questions concerned with **geometry** for example:

- the conditions for congruent triangles;
- enlarging shapes, similar shapes, surface area and volume of similar shapes.

Answers to examples:

1: *AB* = 7.2 cm; *AC* = 12 cm; angle *BCA* = 36.9°
2: volume = 654 cm^3
3: e.g.: (0, 0, 1), but many others
4: a straight line bisecting *AB* at right angles

If you need to revise this subject more thoroughly, see the relevant topics in the *Letts* GCSE *Mathematics Study Guide* or *CD-ROM*.

1   The flag of the Black and White Shipping Company consists of a black rhombus on a white rectangle, as shown in the diagram. The length of the rectangle is 1.6 m, the width is 0.8 m and the rhombus is made by joining the midpoints of the sides.

Calculate the area of material needed to make the black rhombus.

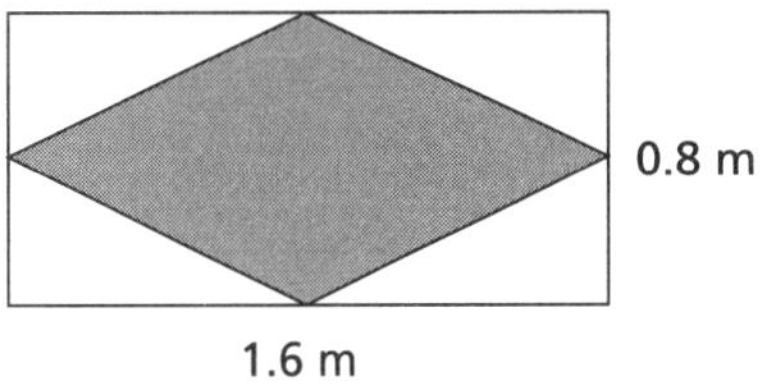

0.8 m

1.6 m

....

....

Answer _____ m^2 (3)

2   The logo for a company consists of 2 small circles inside a larger circle, as shown. The two inside circles have radii of 2 cm and 3 cm.

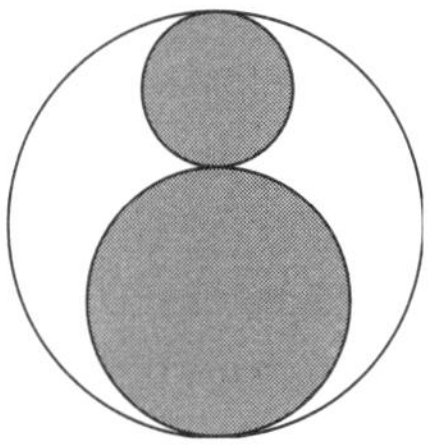

(a) Find the radius of the large circle.

....

Answer _____ cm (2)

(b) Find the shaded area.

....

....

Answer _____ cm^2 (3)

3   Two circular discs are cut out of a rectangular sheet of metal. What is the area of metal left?

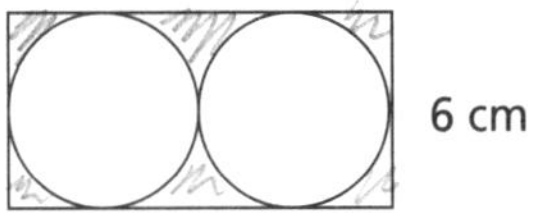

6 cm

12cm

....

Answer _____ cm^2 (5)

4 The bottom of this swimming pool slopes evenly from a depth of 2 m at the shallow end to 4 m at the deep end.

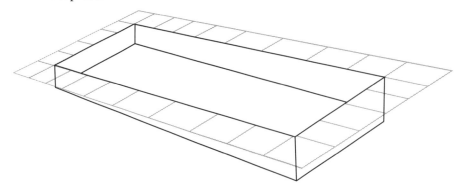

The pool is 25 m long and 15 m wide. Find its volume.

....

....

Answer _____ m³ (4)

5 Some of the expressions shown in the table below can be used to calculate areas or volumes of various shapes.

π and 2 are numbers which have no dimensions. The letters r, b, and h represent lengths.

$2\pi r$	πr^2	$2bh$	πr^3	$b^2 h$	$r^2 + b^3$

(a) Put a letter A in the box underneath those expressions which can be used to calculate an area.

(b) Put a letter V in the box underneath those expressions which can be used to calculate a volume.

(3)

ULEAC 1995

6 A semicircle is cut away from a rectangular piece of metal. The rectangle has length $3r$ cm and width $2r$ cm. Find the area of metal remaining.

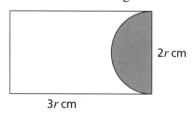

2*r* cm

3*r* cm

....

....

Answer _____ cm² (4)

7

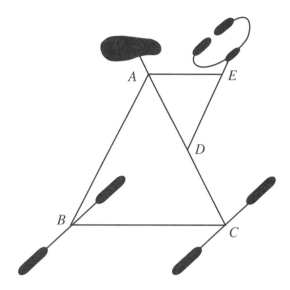

The diagram shows the framework, *ABCDE*, of an exercise bicycle.

In the framework, *AB = AC*, *DA = DE = DC* and *AE* is parallel to *BC*.

(a) Explain why the triangles *ABC* and *ADE* are similar.

.... (2)

(b) The length of the cross-bar *AE* is 35 cm.
Calculate the length of *BC*.

....

Answer _____ cm (2)

NICCEA 1995

8 The diagram shows a running track with the 'straights' 90 m long and with semicircular end sections. If the inside distance is 400 m and the track is 8 m wide, how much further is it to run round the outside of the track?

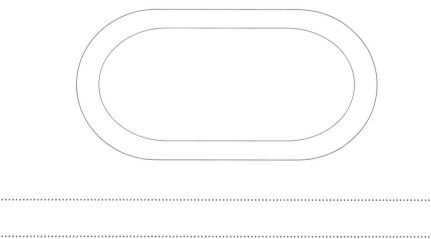

....

....

Answer _____ m (5)

QUESTIONS
9

A new tube of toothpaste is roughly a cylinder, diameter 3.0 cm, length 14.5 cm.

(a) Calculate the volume of toothpaste in the tube.

....

....

Answer _____ cm³ (2)

The toothpaste is squeezed through a circular hole, diameter 7 mm. Each time I clean my teeth, I use a 'cylinder' of length 15 mm.

(b) How many times can I clean my teeth from this tube?

....

....

Answer _____ (4)

10 In a school hall, the stage is lit by a spotlight fixed to a wall.

The spotlight is 4.35 metres up the wall and is set to shine on a spot on the stage 5.2 metres away from the wall, as shown in the diagram.

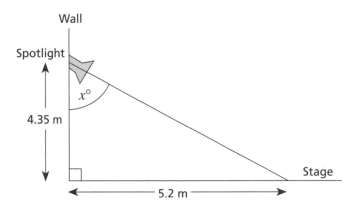

Calculate the size of the angle marked $x°$.

Do not use a scale drawing.

....

....

.... (4)

SEB 1995

11 Find the unknown lengths in these right-angled triangles.

(a)

?   14

8

....

....

....

Answer _____ (3)

(b)

7   ?

6

....

....

Answer _____ (3)

12

DO NOT USE THIS
LADDER AT ANGLES
MORE THAN 70° TO
THE HORIZONTAL

Gurpal's ladder is 5.50 m long.

(a) If it stands on horizontal ground, how far up the wall can it reach?

....

Answer _____ m (3)

(b) How far will the foot of the ladder then be from the wall?

....

Answer _____ m (3)

Mark also has a ladder. Its length can be extended. He puts his ladder with the foot 1.80 m from the wall. It makes an angle of 67° with the ground.

(c) How far up the wall will it reach?

....

....

Answer _____ m (3)

13

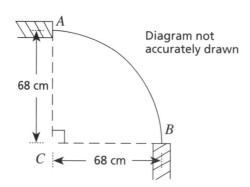

The diagram represents the plan of a window frame.
The arc *AB* is a quarter of a circle.
The centre of the circle is at *C* and the radius of the circle is 68 cm.

(a) Calculate the length of the arc *AB*.

(Use $\pi = 3.14$ or use the π button on your calculator.)
Give your answer correct to 3 significant fiqures.

....

....

Answer _____ cm   (3)

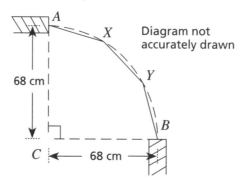

The window frame in part (a) is replaced by double glazed panels.
These panels are made only in straight lengths.
The arc *AB* is replaced by three identical panels *AX*, *XY* and *YB*.

(b) Calculate the length of *AX*.
Give your answer correct to 2 significant figures.

....

....

....

Answers _____ cm   (4)

ULEAC 1995

14

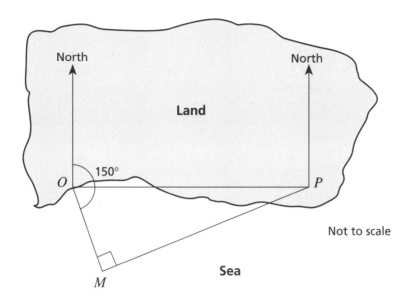

Not to scale

The mast, *M*, of a sunken ship is seen on a bearing of 150° from a point *O* on the coast. A point, *P*, due East of *O*, is such that the angle *OMP* is 90°.

(a) Find the bearing of *M* from *P*.

....

....

Answer Bearing is _____ (3)

(b) Divers decide to search the sea-bed around the ship for treasure. The region they search is a circle, radius 20 metres.

(i) What formula do you need to use to find the area of a circle?

Answer _____ (1)

(ii) Calculate the area of the sea-bed which the divers search.

....

Answer _____ m² (2)

(c) *P* is 100 metres from *O* and *M* is 50 metres from *O*. Use Pythagoras' theorem to calculate the distance *MP*. Give your answer correct to the nearest 0.1 m.

....

....

Answer _____ m (3)

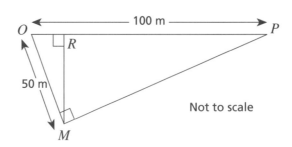

(d) *R* is the point on *OP* nearest to *M*, so that angle *ORM* is 90°

Calculate the distance *MR*.

....

....

Answer _____ m (3)

(e) The points *O* and *P* are at sea level. Taking the axis *Ox* as due East from *O*, axis *Oy* as due North from *O* and axis *Oz* as vertically upwards from *O*, the coordinates of *O* are (0, 0, 0).

There is a lighthouse, 30 metres high, at *P*.

Write down the coordinates of the top of the lighthouse.

....

Answer _____ (2)

MEG 1995

15 Pauline is building a greenhouse.

The base, *PQRS* of the greenhouse should be a rectangle measuring 2.6 m by 1.4 m.

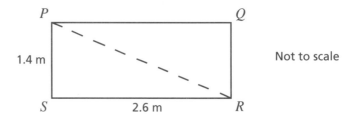

To check the base is rectangular Pauline has to measure the diagonal *PR*.

(a) Calculate the length of *PR* when the base is rectangular.
    You **must** show all your working.

....

....

Answer _____ m (3)

(b) When building the greenhouse Pauline finds angle $PSR > 90°$. She measures PR.

Which of the following statements is **true**?

X: PR is greater than it should be.
Y: PR is less than it should be.
Z: PR is the right length.

Answer _____ (1)

SEG 1995

16

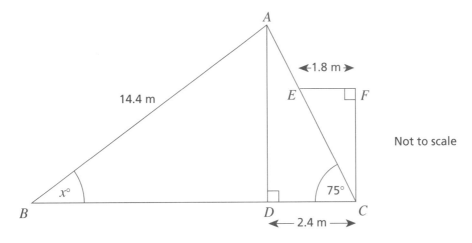

The diagram represents a triangular roof frame ABC with a window frame EFC.

BDC and EF are horizontal and AD and FC are vertical.

(a) Calculate the height AD.

....

....

Answer $AD =$ _____ m (3)

(b) Calculate the size of the angle marked $x°$ in the diagram.

....

....

Answer $x =$ _____ (3)

(c) Calculate FC.

....

....

Answer $FC =$ _____ m (3)

MEG 1995

17 A party of hikers is walking across open moorland using a compass.

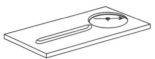

They have been walking on a bearing of 326°. They decide to turn back and retrace their steps.

(a) On what bearing should they walk?

....

Answer _____ (1)

Near the end of the walk there is a steep descent. Lesley decides to check the gradient from the map.

The top has height 293 m and $\frac{1}{2}$ km further on they cross the 150 m contour.

(b) What is the average gradient?

....

Answer _____ (2)

18 This diagram shows a sail *ABDC*.

AC is 4.5m long.
AB is 4.2m long.
Angle *DAC* is 26°.
AD is perpendicular to *BC*.

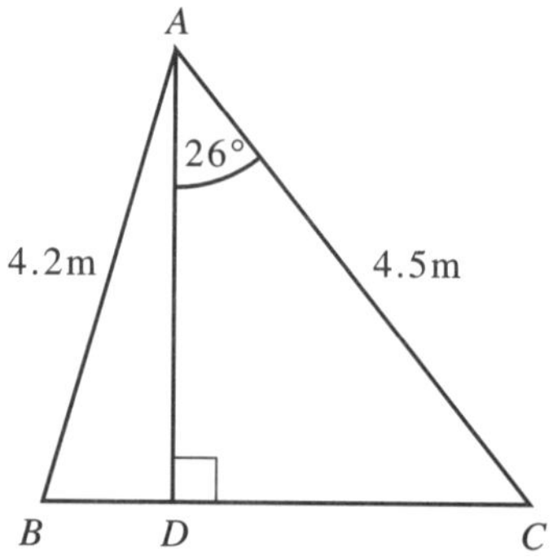

(a) Calculate the height, *AD*, of the sail.

....

....

.... (3)

(b) Calculate angle *ABD*.

....

....

.... (2)

WJEC 1996

19 Here are some expressions associated with a sphere:

$$\tfrac{4}{3}\pi r^3, \quad \pi h^2\left(r - \frac{h}{3}\right), \quad 2\pi rk, \quad 2\pi r^2.$$

(r, h, k are all lengths)

Which of these expressions could be areas? Explain.

....

Answer _____ (2)

20

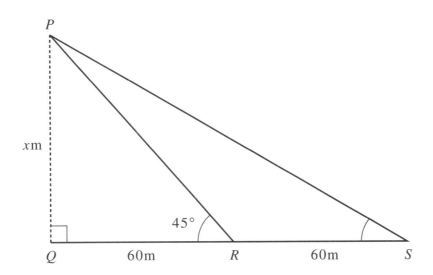

A boat is anchored at point P. Point P is x metres from the beach, QS. Raja walks along the edge of the beach for 60m from point Q to a point R. Angle QRP is 45°.

(a) Write down the value of x

Answer $x =$ _____ (1)

Raja walks for another 60m along the beach to the point S. QS is a straight line.

(b) **Calculate** the size of angle QSP. Give your answer to the nearest degree.

Answer Angle $QSP =$ _____° (3)

ULEAC 1996

21 The diagram shows a wooden
frame for a doorway. The frame
consists of three sides of a rectangle
and a semicircle.

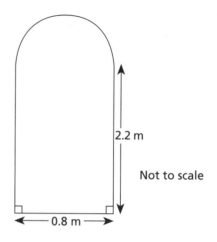

2.2 m

Not to scale

0.8 m

(a) (i) Calculate the length of a semicircle of diameter 0.8 m.

....

Answer _____ m (2)

(ii) Calculate the perimeter of the frame.

Answer _____ m (1)

(b) While the frame was being fitted
into a building it was held in place by supports.

The diagram below shows two of the supports, *AB* and *CD*.
DEA is horizontal.

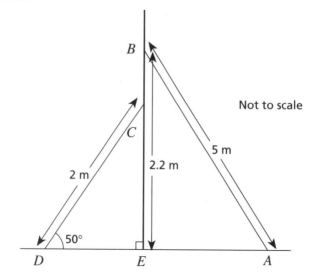

B

Not to scale

C

5 m

2.2 m

2 m

50°

D   *E*   *A*

(i) Calculate the length of *AE*.

....

Answer _____ m (3)

(ii) Calculate the length of *DE*.

....

Answer _____ m (2)

MEG 1995

22 The diagram represents the windscreen wiper on a bus.

P Q

X

A B

Y

It is made of three rigid arms, *PA*, *QB* and *AB*. They are loosely jointed at *A* and *B*. *XY* is the wiper blade and is rigidly fixed to *AB* at right angles.

PA = *QB* and *AB* = *PQ*. *P* and *Q* are pivots fixed to the bus and *PQ* is horizontal. The arm *QB* rotates about *Q* and the arm *PA* rotates about *P*.

(a) Explain why *AB* stays horizontal as *QB* rotates.

.... (1)

(b) Describe the locus of (i) *B* and (ii) *X*.

B ....

X .... (2)

QB rotates in each direction in turn, stopping when it makes an angle of 40° with the vertical.

(c) Sketch the shape wiped by the blade *XY*.

(2)

23 The diagram shows an island drawn to a scale of 1 centimetre to 20 kilometres.

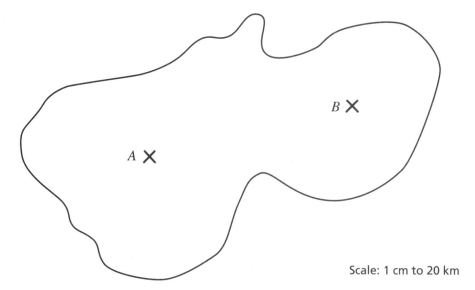

Scale: 1 cm to 20 km

The island has 2 radio transmitters.

The transmitter at *A* has a range of 80 kilometres, which means radio programmes can be heard up to 80 kilometres away from *A*.

The transmitter at *B* has a range of 60 kilometres.

(a) On the diagram above, show as accurately as you can the parts of the island where radio programmes can be heard. (3)

It is planned to build a third transmitter on the island with a range of 20 kilometres.

(b) (i) Mark with an *X* on the diagram the best position for this transmitter. (1)

(ii) Will this transmitter be sufficient to allow all the islanders to hear the radio programmes?

You must explain your answer.

.... (1)

SEB 1995

There are two main sections in this attainment target – **collecting, processing and interpreting data** and **probability**.

Questions involving the **processing and interpreting of information** may include the drawing of graphs – e.g. frequency diagrams and cumulative frequency curves and using these to estimate median and interquartile range, as well as the drawing of bar charts and pie charts. The median and mode, as well as the mean, may, in some questions, have to be calculated.

Example 1: The table shows the heights of 50 eight-year-old boys.
Calculate estimates for (a) the mean height and
(b) the median height of the boys.

Height (h cm)	Number	
$96 \leqslant h < 100$	1	98
$100 \leqslant h < 104$	3	102
$104 \leqslant h < 108$	8	106
$108 \leqslant h < 112$	12	110
$112 \leqslant h < 116$	13	114
$116 \leqslant h < 120$	7	118
$120 \leqslant h < 124$	4	122
$124 \leqslant h < 128$	2	126

Questions concerned with **probability** will extend from straightforward ones such as:

Example 2: Find the probability of drawing a black ball from a bag containing 10 black balls, 15 red balls and 20 green balls.

Example 3: The probability that my train will be late is 0.35.
What is the probability that it will not be late?

to more involved ones:

Example 4: A bag contains 8 red marbles and 6 yellow marbles. Three marbles are taken from the bag at random and not replaced. Find the probability of drawing (a) three red ones, (b) three yellow ones and (c) at least one red marble.

Answers to examples:

1: mean = [98 × 1 + 102 × 3 + …] ÷ 50 = 112.4 cm,
median (between 25th and 26th) is just in the interval $112 \leqslant h < 116$
= 112 cm

2: $\dfrac{2}{9}$

3: 0.65

4: $\dfrac{2}{13}$, $\dfrac{5}{91}$, $\dfrac{86}{91}$

4 Handling data

QUESTIONS

1 Alfalfa (or lucerne) is a plant used for animal fodder and the extraction of chlorophyll. It can be grown in water.

An experiment was conducted, growing alfalfa in various depths of water. The table shows the results:

Depth of water (cm)	30	45	60	75	90	105	120
Yield of alfalfa (tonnes/hectare)	13.1	14.1	15.6	17.8	20.3	21.5	20.8

(a) Draw a scatter diagram for these data. (2)

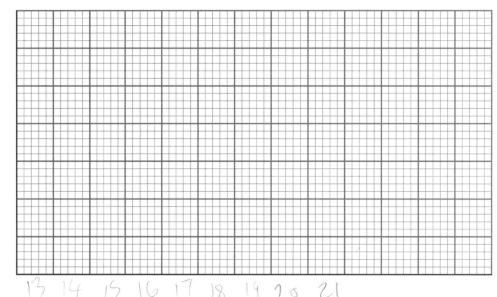

13 14 15 16 17 18 19 20 21

(b) Draw a line of best fit on the diagram. (1)

(c) Estimate the yield for a depth of 100 cm.

Answer _____ tonnes/hectare (1)

(d) Why would you not use your line to estimate the yield at depth 150 cm?

.... (2)

2 The salaries of 8 employees working in a department of a large company are as follows:

£21 000   £23 500   £27 500   £36 000   £19 000   £23 500   £19 000   £19 000

(a) Find the mean, median and mode of their salaries.

....

Mean = £ _____   Median = £ _____   Mode = £ _____ (3)

(b) Which one does not give a good indication of their average salary? Why?

.... (1)

3 John recorded the results of his football team's last 24 matches.

W	W	D	L	W	L	W	D
D	L	L	W	W	W	L	L
D	W	L	W	W	L	W	L

Key:	W	Win
	D	Draw
	L	Lose

(a) Organize and display this information in a table in the space below.

(4)

(b) Janet told John that, since there are three possible results of any match, the probability that the next match would be a draw was $\frac{1}{3}$.

(i) Explain why Janet's argument is wrong.

....

.... (2)

(ii) What might John suggest for the probability of a draw, based on the past performance of his team?

....

Answer _____ (2)

(c) Julia estimates that the probability that her hockey team will win their next match is 0.6 and that the probability they will lose is 0.3.

What is the probability that her team will draw?

....

Answer _____ (2)

(d) Complete the table to show all the possible pairs of results for John's team and Julia's team for their next matches.

John's team	Julia's team
W	W
W	L

(2)

(e) Using John's and Julia's estimates from parts (b) and (c), calculate the probability that John's team and Julia's team will both draw their next match.

....

Answer _____ (2)

MEG 1995

4 (a) A headline in a newspaper this year stated:

Students skip Breakfast!

Our survey shows that few students are eating cereals, fruit, or bread for breakfast.

In fact they eat nothing at all!

You are asked to conduct a survey to find out what students eat for breakfast.

Design an observation sheet to collect the data you need.

Invent the first 20 entries on your data sheet.

(3)

(b) The newspaper made the following statement about the eating habits of teenagers.

> Only one in a hundred teenagers eat fruit and vegetables each day. Over half eat no vegetables other than chips

You are asked to find out whether this statement is true in your area.
Give three questions you could ask teenagers to see if what the article says is true in your area.

....

....

.... (3)

NEAB 1995

5   A historian is comparing the populations of England and Wales in 1881 and 1951.
These are the distributions for the male population (in 1000's):

Age	Mid-value	Number of men 1881	Number of men 1951	Cumulative frequency 1881	Cumulative frequency 1951
Under 15		4740	3785		
15 and under 30		3380	4150		
30 and under 45		2250	4639		
45 and under 60		1430	3722		
60 and under 75		710	2232		
75 and over		110	534		

(Take the mid-value of the '75 and over' group to be 82.5, that is everyone is under 90.)

(a) (i)   Draw the two frequency polygons on the same axes. Label each.

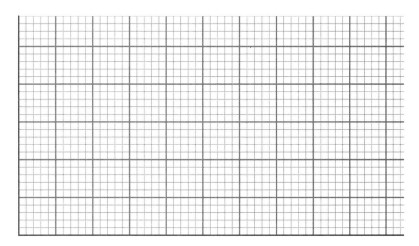

(4)

(ii) Calculate the mean ages in 1881 and 1951.

....

Mean age (1881) _____ (2)

....

Mean age (1951) _____ (2)

(iii) Comment on the differences between the two distributions.

.... (2)

(b) (i) Use the spare columns to write down the cumulative frequencies. (2)

   (ii) Draw the cumulative frequency curves on the same axes below. Label each. (4)

(c) Use the curves to find, for each year,

   (i) the median ages,

   (ii) the interquartile ranges,

   (iii) the percentages of the male populations over 21.

....

Answers:

	Median	IQ range	% over 21
1881			
1951			

(6)

(d) Comment on any other differences.

.... (2)

6 Ten people entered a craft competition.

Their displays of work were awarded marks by two different judges.

Competitor	A	B	C	D	E	F	G	H	I	J
First Judge	90	35	60	15	95	25	5	100	70	45
Second Judge	75	30	55	20	75	30	10	85	65	40

The table shows the marks that the two judges gave to each of the competitors.

(a) (i) On the grid below, draw a scatter diagram to show this information.

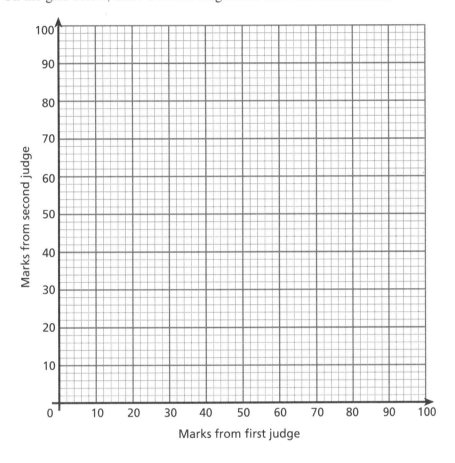

(3)

(ii) Draw a line of best fit. (1)

(b) A late entry was given 75 marks by the first judge.

Use your scatter diagram to estimate the mark that might have been given by the second judge. (Show how you found your answer.)

....

.... (2)

NEAB 1995

7 A survey was made of the time spent by each of 500 customers at the check-outs of a supermarket. The results were recorded in the frequency table.

Time (t minutes)	Frequency
$0 < t \leqslant 1$	83
$1 < t \leqslant 2$	138
$2 < t \leqslant 3$	141
$3 < t \leqslant 4$	68
$4 < t \leqslant 5$	45
$5 < t \leqslant 6$	25

(a) Calculate the mean time spent by each customer at the check-out.

....

Answer _____ minutes (4)

(b) Complete the cumulative frequency table.

Time (less than or equal to) minutes	Cumulative frequency
1	83
2	
3	
4	
5	
6	

(3)

(c) Draw the cumulative frequency curve on the graph paper on the next page. (4)

(d) Use the graph to estimate

  (i) the median time,

Answer _____ minutes (1)

  (ii) the interquartile range.

Answer _____ minutes (2)

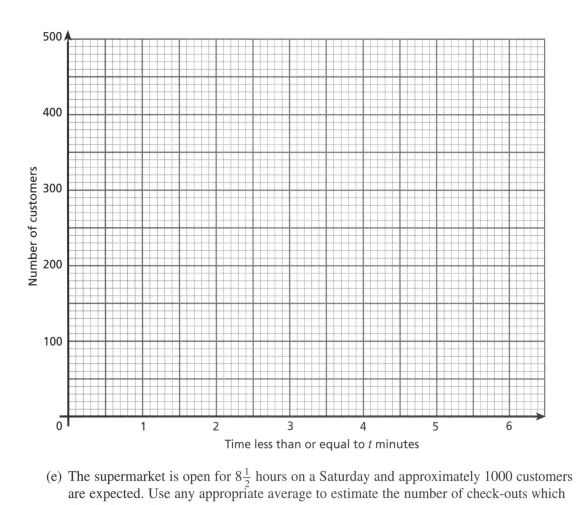

Number of customers

Time less than or equal to *t* minutes

(e) The supermarket is open for $8\frac{1}{2}$ hours on a Saturday and approximately 1000 customers are expected. Use any appropriate average to estimate the number of check-outs which should be used.

....

....

Answer _____ check-outs

Average used _____ (3)

NICCEA 1995

8 A card is selected at random from an ordinary pack of 52 playing cards.

(a) What is the probability of selecting either a red king or a red queen?

....

Answer _____ (1)

The pack of cards now has all the jacks, queens and kings removed.

(b) What is the probability of drawing a black six from the remaining cards?

....

Answer _____ (1)

9 John makes a spinner game for the school fete. When the pointer is spun the probabilities of scoring a colour or a number are given on the table below.

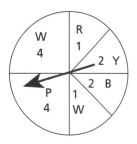

Colour	Probability		Number	Probability
white	0.375		1	0.25
purple	0.25		2	0.25
red	0.125		4	0.5
yellow	0.125			
blue	0.125			

(a) Find the probability of scoring either a 1 or a 4.

....

Answer _____ (2)

(b) Find the probability of getting a purple or a red.

....

Answer _____ (2)

(c) Why is the probabilty of spinning a 1 or a white not 0.25 + 0.375?

.... (3)

10 Little Amy has two spinners, one with four sides, numbered 1, 2, 3, 4 and the other with six sides numbered 1, 2, 3, 4, 5, 6.

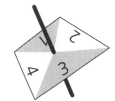
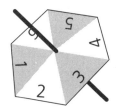

She spins both of them.

(a) List all the possible outcomes.

....

.... (2)

(b) Make a table showing the sum of the two numbers for each outcome.

(2)

(c) What is the probability that

   (i) the sum is 5,   (ii) the sum is odd?

....

Answers: (i) _____ (1)

(ii) _____ (1)

Amy's elder brother Richard thinks that the probability of the sum being either 5 or an odd number can be found by adding the two previous answers.

(d) Explain why he is wrong.

.... (1)

(e) How can you work out the probability that the sum is even without using the table?

.... (1)

11 The table shows the number of 999 calls received in one area:

Police	83
Ambulance	92
Fire	16
Coastguard	4

Based on these data, what is the probability that the next call received is for

(a) an ambulance,   (b) fire or the coastguard?

....

....

Answers: (a) _____ (1)

(b) _____ (2)

QUESTIONS

12 A pack of 52 playing cards consists of equal numbers of clubs, diamonds, hearts and spades.

Ten cards are removed from the pack and placed face down on a table.

When one of these cards is taken at random the following probabilities apply:

Type of card	Probability
club	0.4
diamond	0.2
heart	0.1
spade	0.3

Number on card	Probability
2	0.2
3	0.2
4	0.1
5	0.3
7	0.2

Four of the ten cards are clubs.

They are numbered 2, 4, 5 and 7.

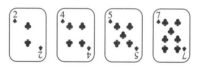

One of the ten cards is taken from the table at random.

(a) What is the probability that it is **not** a diamond?

Answer _____ (1)

(b) What is the probability that it is a club or a diamond?

Answer _____ (1)

(c) What is the probability that it is a club or numbered 3?

....

Answer _____ (2)

(d) Explain why the probability that it is a club or numbered 5 is **not** 0.4 + 0.3.

....

.... (2)

SEG 1995

13

A target has a bull's-eye worth 10 points, and an outer ring worth 3 points.

Siobahn fires an arrow at the target.

The probability that she misses the target completely is $\frac{1}{9}$.

The probability that she hits the bull's eye and scores 10, is $\frac{2}{9}$.

The probability that she hits the outer ring and scores 3, is $\frac{2}{3}$.

Siobahn fires two arrows.

(a) Calculate the probability that Siobahn fails to score with her two arrows.

....

Answer _____ (2)

(b) Calculate the probability that she scores a total of 13 points.

....

Answer _____ (3)

(c) Calculate the probability that she scores **either** no points **or** 6 points with her two arrows.

....

....

Answer _____ (3)

SEG 1995

Answers

1 NUMBER

Question	Answer	Mark
1	$733.60 - 40 \times 7.30 = 441.60$	1
	$441.60 \div 36.80 = 12$	1

Examiner's tip It is not necessary to write down the intermediate step but it is a good idea to do so in case you make an error in the second step.

Question	Answer	Mark
2	$\dfrac{4.7 - 3.6}{3.6} \times 100$	1
	$= 30.55555555... = 30.6\%$	1

Examiner's tip Most calculators require you to key = before ÷ 3.6. It is better to round your answer than leave a string of decimals. You could argue for the answer to be given as 31 as the data was given to two significant figures.

Question	Answer	Mark
3	$\dfrac{7000 \times 400}{60\,000\,000} \times 100$	1
	$= 4.7\%$ or 5%	1

Examiner's tip The data given is already approximate so no rounding is needed until the final answer. This has been given to 1 or 2 significant figures, although only one significant figure is justified by 1significant figure data.

Question	Answer	Mark
4	$\dfrac{12\,800 - 12\,400}{12\,800} \times 100$	1
	$= 3.125\%$	1

Examiner's tip In this question the amount was reduced but it is still the starting value that appears under the fraction.

Question	Answer	Mark
5	I increased by 10% means it is multiplied by 1.10	1
	R increased by 20% means it is multiplied by 1.20	1
	$V = IR$ is multiplied by $1.1 \times 1.2 = 1.32$	1
	V is increased by 32%	1

Examiner's tip Using multipliers is the easiest way to tackle this sort of problem.

Question	Answer	Mark
6	$P = \sqrt{\dfrac{4.6 \times 10^6}{2.8 \times 10^2}} = 128.173\,9889$	1
	$= 1.28 \times 10^2 \text{ or } 1.3 \times 10^2$	1

> **Examiner's tip** Notice that there is a mark for getting the calculation right even if it is not in standard form. Your calculator may not show as many digits as this.

7 (a)	5×10^9	1
(b)	$\dfrac{4 \times 10^{11}}{5 \times 10^9}$	1
	$= 8 \times 10$	1

8 (a) (i) 0.021 358 613 (ii) 0.0214 or 0.021		2+1

> **Examiner's tip** This is firstly a test to see if you can use your calculator correctly. A common error is to multiply by 6.81 rather than divide by it. The decision about the answer to (ii), in the absence of other information, is based on the number of figures in each item. In this case two are given to 3 significant figures and it is reasonable to keep to this, or one less, in your answer.

(b)	3.9024	2

> **Examiner's tip** This again is to test your ability to use the calculator. It is more efficient to use brackets or the memory than write down an intermediate answer. In all calculator questions it is a good idea to check your answer, either by doing it again, preferably a different way, or by making an estimate to see if your answer is about right.

9 (a)	$\dfrac{1764 - 1575}{1575} \times 100$	1
	$= 12\%$	1
(b)	Interest over 12 months nearly £200	1
	Interest over 24 months nearly £400, about twice as much.	1

> **Examiner's tip** A useful guide in this sort of question is to round the numbers so that you can work it out in your head. In this case you might have preferred to use more accurate estimates, such as £190 and £380. There is no need to work out the rate of interest. You can, of course, check it on your calculator, unless the question is asked in a section in which calculators are not permitted.

Question	Answer	Mark
10 (a)	65	1
(b)	67.5, 62.5	1+1
(c)	No — the upper bound on the balance is 62.5 which is less than the lower bound on the scales.	1
	The scales and the electronic scales could both be right since 65 < 67.5.	1

11	$s = \dfrac{25.0^2 - 50.0^2}{2 \times {}^-9.8}$	2
	$= 95.7$ or 96 (95.663 265 31)	1

Examiner's tip Care needs to be taken with the negative sign when you divide by $^-9.8$, most calculators requiring you to key $\pm$ after entering 9.8.

12 (a)	(i)	$18.60 \div 0.496$	1
		$= 37.5$	1
	(ii)	$37.5 \times (0.524 - 0.496)$	1
		$= \pounds1.05$	1
(b)		$1430 \times \dfrac{7}{11}$	1
		$= \pounds910$	1

Examiner's tip Care is needed in part (a) to use consistent units, either both in pounds, as here, or both in pence. However, the answer to part (ii) is better given in pounds.

13	31/12/90: Amount owing $= 650 \times 1.06 - 243 = \pounds446$	1
	31/12/91: Amount owing $= 446 \times 1.06 - 243 = \pounds229.76$	1
	31/12/92: Amount owing $= 229.76 \times 1.06 - 243 = \pounds0.55$	1

Examiner's tip The final answer has been written correct to the nearest penny.

14 (a)	$(5 \times 12 + 3) \div 0.394$	1
	$= 160$	1
(b)	63.5	1

Examiner's tip The answer to part (a) is 159.898... and a sensible degree of accuracy here is three significant figures, which is the nearest centimetre.
In part (b) the nearest hundred grams has been used. A person's weigtht may fluctuate during the day.

Question	Answer	Mark
15 (a)	1124×0.85	1
	$= 955.4...$	1
	$= 955$	1
(b)	P: No (975.36)	1
	Q: Yes (782.32)	1
	R: Yes (878.84)	1
	S: No (1036.32)	1

Examiner's tip You can convert 955 kg to 18.8 cwt and then compare weights in cwt.

(c)	$\frac{1030}{1220} \times 100$	2
	$= 84.4\%$	1
	Yes	1

16	8 stones 6 pounds $= 8\frac{6}{14} = 8.428\,571...$ stones	1
	Weight in kg $= 8.428\,571 \div 0.157$	1
	$= 53.68...$	1
	$= 53.7$	1

Examiner's tip You could argue that the weight could be measured to the nearest 10 g instead.

Question	Answer	Mark
17 (a) (i)	$\frac{300}{200} \times 520\,000$	1+1
	$= 780\,000$	1
(ii)	$\frac{1}{8} \times 520\,000$	1+1
	$= 65\,000$	1
(b)	$12.99 \div 0.68$	1
	$= \$19.10$	1

Examiner's tip Take care to notice which way the exchange rate is given and use common sense to check your answer. For example, the number of dollars is greater than the equivalent number of pounds.

2 ALGEBRA

Question	Answer	Mark
1 (a)	$(6 \times 7) + 4$	1
(b)	$(8 \times 9) + 6$	1

Question	Answer	Mark
(c)	$(n + 2)(n + 3) + n$	1
	$n^2 + 2n + 3n + 6 + n$	1
	$n^2 + 6n + 6$	1

> **Examiner's tip** 'Simplify your answer' means that you are expected to collect like terms, in this case that means adding together all the n terms.

Question	Answer	Mark
2 (a) (i)	38, 51	1
(ii)	The differences between terms are successive odd numbers, so the next term will be 51 + the next odd number, 15.	1
(b) (i)	n^2	1
(ii)	Each term is 2 more than the term in the sequence in (b)(i).	1
	$n^2 + 2$	1

> **Examiner's tip** You can find this nth term using the differences noted in part (a) but the question has been arranged to help you spot the connection between the sequence and the more familiar square numbers.

Question	Answer	Mark
3 (a) (i)	$\sqrt{\left(10^2 + 24^2\right)}$	1
	$= 26$	1
(ii)	$\sqrt{\left(12^2 + 35^2\right)}$	1
	$= 37$	1
(b) (i)	22	1
(ii)	48	1
(c) (i)	$2 + 2n$ or $2(n + 1)$	2
(ii)	If $n = 1$, $1^2 + k = 3$, $k = 2$	1

> **Examiner's tip** Notice that sequence p is the even numbers but not starting with 2. This gives a clue to finding the nth term. In part (c)(ii), you can use any value of n to find k. For example, $n = 5$, $25 + 5k = 35$ also gives $k = 2$.

Question	Answer	Mark
4 (a)	$6x^2 + 21x - 12x - 42$	1
	$6x^2 + 9x - 42$	1

> **Examiner's tip** This could be written as $3(2x^2 + 3x - 14)$.

Question	Answer	Mark
(b) (i)	$(x + 3)(x - 2)$	2

> **Examiner's tip** The '+x' in the expression means that it will be '+3' and '−2' in the brackets.

Question	Answer	Mark
(ii)	$x = {}^-3$ or $x = 2$	1+1

Question	Answer		Mark
5 (a)	$21 - 3x = 4x$	(adding 10 to both sides)	1
	$21 = 7x$	(adding $3x$ to both sides)	1
	$x = 3$	(dividing both sides by 7)	1
(b)	$x = 2 \qquad x^3 = 8$	(reasonably close trial)	1
	$\qquad 1.9 \qquad\quad 6.859$		
	$\qquad 1.95 \qquad 7.4148...$		
	$\qquad 1.92 \qquad 7.0778...$	(just too big)	1
	$\qquad 1.91 \qquad 6.9678...$	(just too small)	1
	$\qquad 1.915 \qquad 7.0227...$		
	1.915 is too big so 1.91 is correct to 2 decimal places.		1

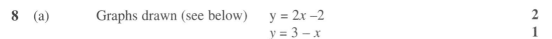

> **Examiner's tip** Since the value when $x = 1.92$ is much further from 7 than the value when $x = 1.91$, it is sufficient to give this as your reason for choosing 1.91.

Question	Answer	Mark
6 (a)	$^{-}1, 0, 1, 2, 3, 4, 5$	3
(b)	$2x^4$	3
(c)	$15y^2 + 18y - 20y - 24 + 10$	1
	$15y^2 - 2y - 14$	2

> **Examiner's tip** There will be part marks for partly correct answers. Full marks will only be available for fully simplified answers.

Question	Answer	Mark
7 (a)	$3n - 4 < 17$	1
(b)	$3n < 17 + 4$	1
	$n < 7$	1

> **Examiner's tip** Although solving this inequality looks much the same as solving the equation $3n - 4 = 18$, it is important to keep the inequality sign the right way round. In some cases this will not be so obvious.

Question	Answer		Mark
8 (a)	Graphs drawn (see below)	$y = 2x - 2$	2
		$y = 3 - x$	1

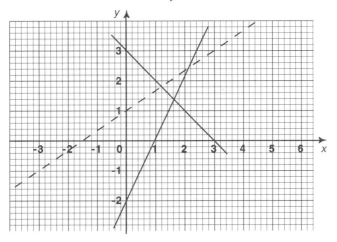

Question	Answer	Mark
(b)	$x = 1.7$, y $= 1.3$	1

9

$2x + 3y = 17$ ....(i)
$3x - 2y = 6$.................(ii)   number the equations for identification
(i) times 3 gives $6x + 9y = 51$.............(iii)
(ii) times 2 gives $6x - 4y = 12$.............(iv)
subtract: $13y = 39$ **1**
therefore $y = 3$ **1**
substitute in (i) gives: $2x + 9 = 17$ **1**
$2x = 8$
$x = 4$ **1**

10

$s = 10 \times 11 \times 21 \div 6$ **1**
$= 385$ **1**

11 (a)

$Q = 3600 \times 12 \times 2 \div 55$ **1**
$= 1570(.909...)$ **1**

(b)

$1000 = 3600 \times 15 \times N \div 120$ **1**
$N = 1000 \times 120 \div 3600 \div 15$ **1**
$= 2.2...$, i.e. 3 lanes.   **1**

12

$F = 2C$ **1**
$C = \frac{5}{9}(2C - 32)$ (substituting for F)   **1**
$9C = 10C - 160$ (multiplying by 9 and expanding the bracket)   **1**
$-C = -160$ (subtracting $10C$ from both sides)
$C = 160$ **1**

Question	Answer	Mark
13	Mean $= (30 + 40 + x + 50 + 80) \div 5 = 40 + \dfrac{x}{5}$	1
	Median $= x$	1
	$40 + \dfrac{x}{5} = x$	1
	$\dfrac{4}{5}x = 40$ (subtracting $\dfrac{x}{5}$ from both sides)	1
	$x = 50$ (multiplying by 5 and dividing by 4)	1

Examiner's tip You can be asked to form an equation before solving it.

Question	Answer	Mark
14 (a)	$3d + 7w = 53.4$	1
	$d + 10w = 50$	1
(b)	$3d + 30w = 150$ (multiplying second equation by 3)	1
	$3d + 7w = 53.4$ (first equation)	
	$23w = 96.6$ (subtracting the equations)	1
	$w = 4.2$ (dividing by 23)	1
	$d = 50 - 10 \times 4.2 = 8$ (substituting in second equation)	1

Question	Answer	Mark
15	0, 1, 2, 3	2

Examiner's tip Notice that ⁻1 is not included as the numbers must be greater than it. However 3 is included as that inequality sign includes 'equals'.

Question	Answer	Mark
16 (a)	$3x = 14, x = 4\frac{2}{3}$	1 + 1
(b)	$2x - 1 = 7, 2x = 8$	1
	$x = 4$	1
(c)	$6x + 3 = 18, 6x = 15$	1
	$x = 2\frac{1}{2}$	1

Examiner's tip There are other ways to solve such equations, e.g., in part (b), multiply out the bracket: $10x - 5 = 35, 10x = 40$.

Question	Answer	Mark
17	$20 = \sqrt{\dfrac{2 \times 3950 \times h}{5280}}$	1
	$h = \dfrac{20^2 \times 5280}{2 \times 3950}$	1
	$= 267(.34...)$	1

Question	Answer	Mark

You could also rearrange the formula before substituting. The formula would be

$$h = \frac{5280D^2}{2r}$$

18	$PV = k$ (multiplying both sides by V)	1
	$V = \dfrac{k}{P}$ (dividing both sides by P)	1

Examiner's tip It is safer to do this in two simple steps.

19 (a)	$2x \leqslant 15$ (adding 7 to both sides)	
	$x \leqslant 7\frac{1}{2}$ (dividing both sides by 2)	1
(b)	$^-x > ^-1$ (subtracting 3 from both sides)	
	$x < 1$ (dividing both sides by $^-1$ and changing sign)	1

Examiner's tip It is important to notice that if you change the signs of the two sides of an inequality, in this case from negative to positive, it is necessary to change the inequality sign also. For example, $7 > 4$ but $^-7 < ^-4$.

You can do it another way:

    $3 > 2 + x$ (adding x to both sides)
    $1 > x$ (subtracting 2 from both sides)
    $x < 1$ (writing from right to left)

(c)	$x^2 < 4$ (subtracting 4 from both sides)	
	If $x > 0$, $x < 2$ (taking positive square root)	1
	If $x < 0$, $x > ^-2$ (taking negative square root and therefore changing inequality sign)	1

Examiner's tip These two inequalities can be combined as $^-2 < x < 2$.

20	$x = 2.5$	$2.5^3 - 2.5 = 13.125$	Too small	1
	$x = 2.7$	$2.7^3 - 2.7 = 16.983$	Too big	1
	$x = 2.6$	$2.6^3 - 2.6 = 14.976$	Nearest	1

Examiner's tip To get closer to the solution systematically, it is useful to take a value between the two that were "too big" and "too small", 2.5 between 2 and 3, 2.7 between 2.5 and 3 and 2.6 between 2.5 and 2.7.

Question	Answer	Mark
21 (a)	Area $= y^2 - 4 \times \frac{1}{2}x^2$	1
	$= y^2 - 2x^2$	1
(b)	$x^2 + x^2 = 14^2$ (applying Pythagoras to any corner triangle)	1
	$2x^2 = 196$	
	$x^2 = 98$	1
	$x = 9.899...$	1

Examiner's tip Although not a sensible degree of accuracy for a practical problem, keep all the figures on your calculator for the next calculations.

(c)	$y = 14 + 2x = 33.798...$	1
	Area $= 33.798^2 - 2 \times 9.899^2$	
	$= 946 \, cm^2$	1

Examiner's tip In this case, had you used the rounded answers $x = 9.0$ and $y = 33.8$ you would have still obtained the above answer but that is not always so – only round at the end.

Question	Answer	Mark
22 (a)	$3x - x = 7 + 2$	1
	$x = 4\frac{1}{2}$	1
(b)	$15x + 25y = 76$ (second equation)	
	$\underline{15x + 15y = 60}$ (multiplying first equation by 15)	
	$10y = 16$ (subtracting)	1
	$y = 1.6$	1
	$x = 2.4$	1
(c)	$6x < 15$	1
	$x < 2\frac{1}{2}$	1
(d)	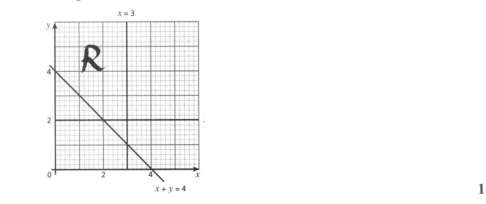	1

Examiner's tip There are other ways to tackle these equations, for instance, in part (b), multiply the first equation by 25 and subtract, giving $10x = 24$. To check the correct region in part (d), choose a point in the region and see if the coordinates satisfy all the inequalities.

Question	Answer	Mark
23	A: Cycling at constant speed	1
	B: Slowing down (going uphill)	1
	C: Accelerating (going downhill)	1
	D: Maximum speed (bottom of hill)	1

Examiner's tip Do not be deceived into thinking that when the graph goes up it is a hill! It actually means the cyclist is going faster, so it is more likely to be down a hill.

24 (a)	80 seconds	1
(b)	10 metres	1
(c)	Robert — steeper graph	1

Examiner's tip Do not be confused by the point where the swimmers cross (going in opposite directions) after 47 seconds.

25 (a) and (b)

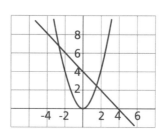

Straight line **1**
Curve **2**

(c) (i) 1.6, ⁻2.6   **1+1**

Examiner's tip You cannot read a hand-drawn graph more accurately than this.

(ii) $x = 1.6$ $x^2 + x - 4 =$

	x	$x^2 + x - 4 =$	
	1.6	0.16	
	1.55	− 0.0475	
	1.57	0.0349	
	1.56	− 0.0064	1
	1.56 is closer		1
	− 2.6	0.16	
	− 2.5	− 0.25	
	− 2.57	0.0349	
	− 2.56	− 0.0064	1
	− 2.56 is closer		1

Examiner's tip You should not need many trials as the starting point was quite accurate.

Question	Answer	Mark

26 (a) and (b)

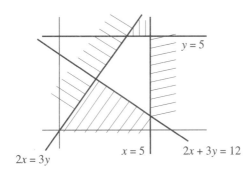

$2x = 3y$ $x = 5$ $2x + 3y = 12$ $y = 5$

4

Examiner's tip If you shade the regions which are **not** included it will be easier to look for possible solution points, should they be asked for.

27

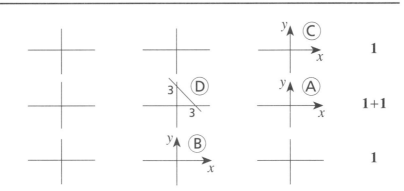

1

1+1

1

28 (a)   Area of square $= x^2$ 1

Area of triangle $= \frac{1}{2} \times 0.5 \times x$ 1

Total area $= x^2 + \frac{1}{4}x$ 1

(b)   Volume $= 4x \times$ area   1

$= 4x^3 + x^2$ 1

So $4x^3 + x^2 = 10$ 1

(c) $x = 1$ $4x^3 + x^2 = 5$

$x = 2$ $4x^3 + x^2 = 36$ 1

$x = 1.5$ $4x^3 + x^2 = 15.75$

$x = 1.25$ $4x^3 + x^2 = 9.375$ 1

$x = 1.3$ $4x^3 + x^2 = 10.478$ 1

Result 1.3   1

Examiner's tip If greater accuracy was required in part (c), the next step would be to find the value when $x = 1.275$ and 1.28.

3 SHAPE AND SPACE

Question	Answer	Mark
1	Area of rhombus is half area of rectangle	1
	Area $= \frac{1}{2} \times 1.6 \times 0.8$	1
	$= 0.64$	1

> **Examiner's tip** An alternative method is to divide the rhombus into four right-angled triangles, using the diagonals.

2 (a)	Radius $= \frac{1}{2} \times (4 + 6)$	1
	$= 5$	1
(b)	Area $= \pi \times 2^2 + \pi \times 3^2$	2
	$= 40.8$	1

> **Examiner's tip** You will have to remember the formula for the area of a circle, πr^2

3	Area of rectangle $= 6 \times 12$	1
	$= 72$	1
	Area of circles $= 2 \times \pi \times 3^2$	1
	$= 56.5...$	1
	Area left $= 72 - 56.5... = 15.45$ or 15.5	1

> **Examiner's tip** You do not need to write down the intermediate answers but it is wise to show how you did the calculation in case you make an error. The marks for your method could still be given.

4	The pool is a prism whose cross section is a trapezium.	1
	Area of cross section $= \frac{1}{2} \times 25 \times (2 + 4)$	1
	$= 75$	1
	Volume $= 15 \times 75 = 1125$	1

> **Examiner's tip** The top edge of the pool is horizontal and the sides vertical, so the diagram shows the cross section:

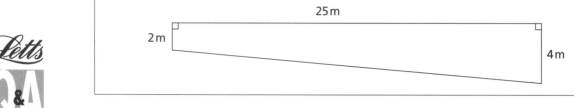

Question	Answer	Mark

5

–	A	A	V	V	–

3

Examiner's tip Notice that π is not a length but a number and $r^2 + b^3$ has mixed dimensions. You will lose a mark for each error.

6

Area of complete rectangle = $3r \times 2r$ 1

           = $6r^2$ 1

Area of semicircle removed = $\frac{1}{2}\pi r^2$ Area required = $6r^2 - \frac{1}{2}\pi r^2$ 1+1

---

7   (a)

Angle EAD = angle ACB, since AE parallel to BC 1

Triangles ABC and DEA isosceles   1

    (b)

$AD = \frac{1}{2}AC$ 1

$BC = 2 \times AE = 70$ cm   1

Examiner's tip Similar triangles have corresponding angles equal as well as proportional sides.

8

Circumference of two inner semicircles = $400 - 2 \times 90 = 220$ 1

Radius of inner semicircles = $220 \div 2\pi = 35.014...$ 1

Radius of outer semicircles = $8 + 35.014... = 43.014...$ 1

Circumference of two outer semicircles = $2 \times \pi \times 43.014 = 270$ 1

Extra distance = $270 - 220 = 50$ 1

Examiner's tip You will need to remember the formula for the circumference of a circle. Notice that the 'straights' are all 90 m long. An answer given to the nearest metre is reasonable in this practical situation.

---

9   (a)

Volume = $\pi \times 1.5^2 \times 14.5$ 1

          = $102.4944...$ 1

    (b)

Volume of toothpaste 'cylinder' = $\pi \times 3.5^2 \times 15 \, \text{mm}^3$ 1

$1 \, \text{cm}^3 = 1000 \, \text{mm}^3$ 1

Number of times = $\dfrac{\pi \times 1.5^2 \times 14.5 \times 1000}{\pi \times 3.5^2 \times 15}$ 1

          = 177 1

Question	Answer	Mark

Don't forget the change of units in part (b). It would not be reasonable to round up the final answer as part of a 'cylinder' is not enough to clean my teeth. In fact the situation is actually more approximate, since toothpaste tubes are not cylinders, but the wording of the question tells you to take it as a cylinder.

10 $\tan x = \dfrac{5.2}{4.35}$ 1+1

$x = 50.08\ldots$ 1
$= 50.1$ or 50 1

Take care you show how you did the calculation, even though it was all done on the calculator. It is sensible not to leave too many figures in the answer in this practical situation.

11 (a) $? = \sqrt{14^2 + 8^2}$ 2

$= 16.12\ldots$ 1

This is the easiest case when using Pythagoras.

(b) $? = \sqrt{7^2 - 6^2}$ 2

$= 3.6055\ldots$ 1

This is the rearranged form, deriving from $7^2 = 6^2 + ?^2$. This question is not set in a practical context so the number of digits in your answer is not important, so long as there are enough to show you have done it correctly, e.g., 16.1 and 3.61 would be perfectly acceptable.

12 (a) $5.50 \sin 70° = 5.168\ldots$ 2
$= 5.17$ 1

(b) $5.50 \cos 70° = 1.881\ldots$ 2
$= 1.88$ 1

You need to realize that the angle to use is on the safety notice, since 'how far **can** it reach' implies maximum angle, which is 70°.

(c) $1.8 \tan 67°$ 2
$= 4.24$ 1

It is reasonable to give 2 decimal places in your answers since this was the accuracy of the data.

Question	Answer	Mark
13 (a)	$2\pi \times 68 \quad = 427.2\ldots$	1
	$427.2 \div 4 = 106.8\ldots$	1
	$= 107$ (to 3 significant figures)	1

(b)

Angle $ACD = \frac{1}{2} \times 30 = 15°$ — 1

$AD = 68\sin 15°$ — 1

$\quad = 17.5\ldots$ — 1

$AX = 2 \times AD = 35$ (2 s.f.) — 1

A, D, X, C figure

Examiner's tip You need to remember the formula for the circumference of a circle in part (a) and realize that the triangle ACX is isosceles to start the solution to part (b).

14 (a)	Angle $OPM = 90° - 60° = 30°$	1
	Bearing $= 270° - 30°$	1
	$= 240°$	1
(b) (i)	πr^2	1
(ii)	$\pi \times 20^2$	1
	$= 1256.6\ldots$ or 1257	1
(c)	$PM^2 = 100^2 - 50^2$	1
	$PM = \sqrt{(100^2 - 50^2)}$	1
	$= 86.6$	1
(d)	$\dfrac{MR}{50} = \dfrac{PM}{100}$	1
	$MR = \dfrac{50}{100} \times 86.6 = 43.3$	1+1
	or $MR = 50\sin 60°$	
	$= 43.3$	
(e)	$(100, 0, 30)$	2

Examiner's tip Part (d) is solved using similar triangles and proportion.

15 (a)	$PR^2 = 1.4^2 + 2.6^2$	1
	$PR = \sqrt{(1.4^2 + 2.6^2)}$	1
	$= 2.95$	1
(b)	X is true	1

Question	Answer	Mark

16 (a) $\tan 75° = \dfrac{AD}{2.4}$ **1**

$AD = 2.4 \times \tan 75°$ **1**

$= 8.96$ **1**

(b) $\sin x = \dfrac{8.96}{14.4}$ **1+1**

$x = 38.5°$ **1**

(c) $FC = 1.8 \tan 75°$ $\dfrac{FC}{AD} = \dfrac{1.8}{2.4}$ **1**

$FC = AD \times \dfrac{1.8}{2.4}$ **1**

$= 6.72$ **1**

17 (a)   146°   **1**

(b)   Average gradient $= \dfrac{293 - 150}{500}$ **1**

$= 0.286$ **1**

18 (a) $\dfrac{AD}{4.5} = \cos 26°$ **1**

$AD = 4.5\cos 26°$ **1**

$= 4.04$ **1**

(b) $\sin ABD = \dfrac{4.0445...}{4.2}$ **1**

$ABD = 74.4°$ **1**

Question	Answer	Mark

Examiner's tip Although it is sensible to give the answer to part (a) to no more than three significant figures, do not use this rounded answer in working out part (b).

Keep all the figures in your calculator and divide by 4.2. (If you use $\dfrac{4.04}{4.2}$, you will get 74.1° as the answer to (b).

19	$2\pi rk$, $2\pi r^2$. These could both be areas as they involve length × length.	**1**
	The others involve length × length × length and could be volumes.	**1**

20 (a)	60m	**1**
(b)	$\tan QSP = \dfrac{60}{120}$	**1**
	$QSP = 26.565$	**1**
	$= 27°$ to the nearest degree.	**1**

Examiner's tip Triangle *PQR* is an isosceles right-angled triangle. In part (b) there is a mark for correctly rounding your answer.

21 (a)	(i) $\frac{1}{2} \times \pi \times 0.8$	**1**
	$= 1.26$	**1**
	(ii) $1.26 + 0.8 + 2 \times 2.2$	
	$= 6.46$	**1**
(b)	(i) $AE^2 = 5^2 - 2.2^2$	**1**
	$AE = \sqrt{\left(5^2 - 2.2^2\right)}$	**1**
	$= 4.49$	**1**
	(ii) $DE = 2\cos 50°$	**1**
	$= 1.29$	**1**

Examiner's tip Don't forget to write down your methods as these earn most of the marks.

22 (a)	*ABQP* is a parallelogram so *AB* remains parallel to *PQ*, which is horizontal	**1**
(b)	(i) *B* moves on an arc of a circle radius *QB*	**1**
	(ii) *X* moves on an arc of equal size at a distance *XB* above *B*	**1**

Question	Answer		Mark
(c)			2

23

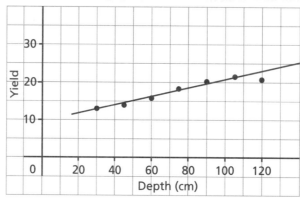

(a)	Circle centre *A* radius 4 cm		1
	Circle centre *B* radius 3 cm		1
	Reception area indicated		1
(b)	(i) *X* marked on part of island not covered		1
	(ii) Yes. Part not covered is less than 20 km long.		1

Examiner's tip In this case only a small part is not covered by *A* and *B*. The third transmitter can be anywhere so long as it is not more than 20 km from the furthest part not covered by *A* and *B*. It is sensible to put it on the island and not in the sea!

4 HANDLING DATA

Question	Answer		Mark
1 (a) and (b)			Plotting points **2**
			Line **1**

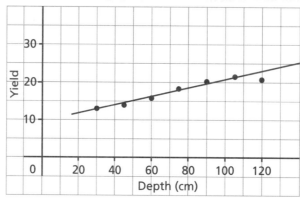

Question	Answer	Mark
(c)	Reading from graph at 100 cm	1
(d)	It is beyond the last depth so we do not know what would happen.	1
	The last reading is lower than the one before it.	1

2 (a)	Mean = £23 562.50	1
	Median = £22 250	1
	Mode = £19 000	1
(b)	The mode – it is the lowest salary paid.	1

3 (a)

Result	Frequency
W	11
D	4
L	9

4

(b)	(i) Not equally likely outcomes	2
	(ii) $\frac{4}{24}$ or $\frac{1}{6}$	2
(c)	$1 - (0.6 + 0.3)$	1
	$= 0.1$	1

(d)

John's team	Julia's team
(W)	(W)
(W)	(L)
W	D
L	W
L	L
L	D
D	W
D	L
D	D

2

Question	Answer	Mark

(e) $0.1 \times \dfrac{1}{6}$ **1**

         $= \dfrac{1}{60}$ or 0.0167 **1**

Examiner's tip Don't get confused between Janet and Julia! In part (e) you would get full credit for an answer which correctly used your earlier answers, even if they were wrong.

4 (a)   **3**

Name	Age	Sex	Cereal	Juice	Fruit	Bread	Cooked
J Smith	16	B	✓	✓	✗	✗	✗

Name	Age	Sex	Cereal	Juice	Fruit	Bread	Cooked
J Jones	17	G	✗	✗	✗	✗	✗

(b)   **1** Did you eat any fruit today?   **1**

         2 Did you eat any vegetables today?   **1**

         3 Did you eat any chips today?   **1**

Examiner's tip Your observation sheet may be very different but it must offer the opportunity to draw various conclusions, having worked out statistics based on the answers to your questions. It is important in part (b) to fix a definite time. You must be able to separate fruit, vegetables and chips to check the statements.

5 (a)   (i)

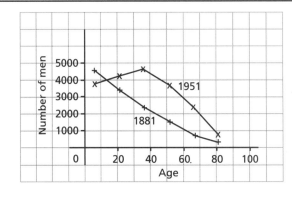

    4
(1 mark deducted for each mistake)

(ii)   Mean (1881) = (7.5 × 4740 + 22.5 × 3380 + etc.) ÷ 12 620   **1**
               = 26.0 years   **1**

      Mean (1951) = (7.5 × 3785 + etc.) ÷ 19 062   **1**
               = 36.0 years   **1**

Examiner's tip If your calculator will do statistics, learn how to use it — it is much quicker! However, do it twice as a check.

Question	Answer	Mark
(iii)	More men in 1951	**1**
	Higher average age in 1951	**1**

Examiner's tip You will also be given credit for other relevant comments, e.g. 'Men lived longer in 1951', 'There were more men over 60 in 1951', etc.

(b) (i)

Cumulative frequencies:	1881	1951	
under 15	4740	3785	
under 30	8120	7935	
under 45	10370	12574	
under 60	11800	16296	
under 75	12510	18528	
under 90	12620	19062	**1+1**

(ii)

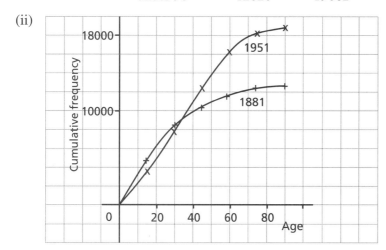

2+2

(1 mark deducted for each mistake)

(c)

	Median	IQ range	% over 21	
1881	20	38 − 10 = 28	50	**1+1+1**
1951	35	50 − 20 = 30	73	**1+1+1**

Examiner's tip Read medians at half total frequency (6310/9531). Read quartiles at 25%/75% of total frequency (3155/9465, 4765/14 296). Subtract readings at 21 years from total frequency and convert to percentages.

(d)	Fewer young men in 1951 (% under 21)	**1**
	Greater spread of ages (interquartile range greater) in 1951	**1**

Examiner's tip There are other possible comments but make sure yours are different from the earlier part. This question is longer than you would be expected to do under examination conditions. In an examination, you would probably not have to repeat calculations, as here, but these were included for practice.

Question	Answer	Mark

6 (a)(i) and (ii)

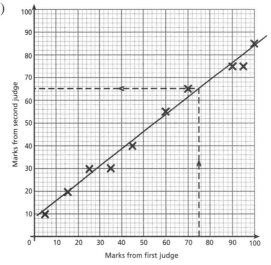

| | | **3** |
| | | Line of best fit **1** |

(b) 65 marks — **1**

Method on diagram — **1**

> **Examiner's tip** One mark in part (b) is for showing your method. It need not be on the diagram, it could be a written description.

7 (a) Mean = $(0.5 \times 83 + 1.5 \times 138 + 2.5 \times 141 + 3.5 \times 68 +$

$4.5 \times 45 + 5.5 \times 25) \div 500$ — **1+1**

$= 1179 \div 500$ — **1**

$= 2.358$ — **1**

(b) (83) 221 362 430 475 500 — **3**

(c)

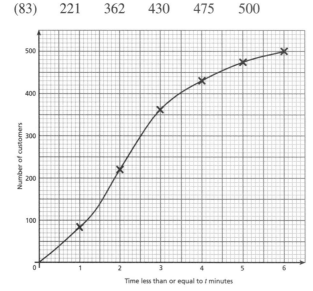

4

(d) (i) 2.2 minutes — **1**

(ii) 3.1 − 1.4 — **1**

= 1.7 minutes — **1**

Question	Answer	Mark
(e)	Mode is 2.5	1
	Average number = (Average time × 1000) ÷ 510	1
	(with mode) = 4.9	
	Needs 5 checkouts	1

Examiner's tip In parts (b) and (c) you will lose marks for errors. Remember to show what you are calculating, even though you use your calculator. In part (e) you could argue for using any average but the mode does make allowance for any peak in the numbers.

---

8 (a) $\dfrac{4}{52} = \dfrac{1}{13}$ (b) $\dfrac{2}{40} = \dfrac{1}{20}$ **1+1**

Examiner's tip Decimal answers are also acceptable, but not ratios or statements such as '1 out of 13'.

---

9 (a)	0.25 + 0.5 = 0.75	2
(b)	0.25 + 0.125 = 0.375	2
(c)	One section contains white and 1.	1
	The probability for white and 1 has been added in twice	2

Examiner's tip The condition that needs to be satisfied before probabilities can be added is sometimes referred to as the outcomes being 'mutually exclusive'.

---

10 (a)

1,1; 1,2; 1,3; 1,4; 1,5; 1,6;

2,1; 2,2; 2,3; 2,4; 2,5; 2,6;

3,1; 3,2; 3,3; 3,4; 3,5; 3,6;

4,1; 4,2; 4,3; 4,4; 4,5; 4,6.   **2**

Examiner's tip The order is important. 1 on the first and 2 on the second is a different outcome from 2 on the first and 1 on the second.

(b)

	1	2	3	4	5	6
1	2	3	4	5	6	7
2	3	4	5	6	7	8
3	4	5	6	7	8	9
4	5	6	7	8	9	10

2

Question	Answer	Mark

(c)　(i)　$\frac{1}{6}$　　　　　　(ii)　$\frac{12}{24} = \frac{1}{2}$　　　　1+1

(d)　5 is also an odd number so the outcomes are not mutually exclusive.　　1

(e)　If the sum is even it is not odd so the probability is $1 - \frac{1}{2} = \frac{1}{2}$　　1

> **Examiner's tip**　The probability of something not happening is 1− (the probability of it happening).

---

11 (a)　$\frac{92}{195}$　　　(b)　$\frac{16+4}{195} = \frac{20}{195} = \frac{4}{39}$　　1+2

> **Examiner's tip**　Since the total number of calls is not given in this question you may assume that it is 195, that is that each call was for only one emergency service.

---

12 (a)　0.8　　1

(b)　0.6　　1

(c)　0.4 + 0.2 = 0.6　　1+1

(d)　One card is both a 5 and a Club *or* not mutually exclusive　　2

> **Examiner's tip**　The answer to part (a) can be found from $1 - 0.2$ or $0.4 + 0.1 + 0.3$. Before answering part (c) you should check that the two outcomes 'It is a Club' and 'It is numbered 3' are mutually exclusive, that is, there is no card that is both a Club and a 3. The question makes this clear.

---

13 (a)　$\frac{1}{9} \times \frac{1}{9} = \frac{1}{81}$ or 0.0123　　1+1

(b)　Bull then outer or outer then bull　　1

$\frac{2}{9} \times \frac{2}{3} + \frac{2}{3} \times \frac{2}{9} = \frac{8}{27}$ or 0.296　　1+1

(c)　Two misses or two outers　　1

$\frac{1}{9} \times \frac{1}{9} + \frac{2}{3} \times \frac{2}{3}$　　1

$= \frac{37}{81}$ or 0.457　　1

> **Examiner's tip**　Firing the two arrows are two independent events, so the probabilities can be multiplied.